True Ghost Stories

REAL DEMONIC POSSESSIONS AND EXORCISMS

BY ZACHERY KNOWLES

Real Haunted Ouija Boards
Copyright © 2016 by Zachery Knowles.

All rights reserved. No part of this book may be reproduced in any form without permission in writing from the author. Reviewers may quote brief passages in reviews

ISBN: 1532712227

ISBN-13: 978-1532712227

Disclaimer

No part of this publication may be reproduced or transmitted in any form or by any means, mechanical or electronic, including photocopying or recording, or by any information storage and retrieval system, or transmitted by email without permission in writing from the publisher.

While all attempts have been made to verify the information provided in this publication, neither the author nor the publisher assumes any responsibility for errors, omissions, or contrary interpretations of the subject matter herein.

This book is for entertainment purposes only. The views expressed are those of the author alone, and should not be taken as expert instruction or commands. The reader is responsible for his or her own actions.

Adherence to all applicable laws and regulations, including international, federal, state, and local governing professional licensing, business practices, advertising, and all other aspects of doing business in the US, Canada, or any other jurisdiction is the sole responsibility of the purchaser or reader.

Neither the author nor the publisher assumes any responsibility or liability whatsoever on the behalf of the purchaser or reader of these materials.

Any perceived slight of any individual or organization is purely unintentional.

YOUR FREE GIFT

As a way of saying thanks for your purchase, I'm offering a free eBook to readers of my *True Ghost Stories* series.

To instantly download the PDF version of my book, *Real Black-Eyed Kids*, all you need to do is visit:

<u>www.realhorror.net</u>

CONTENTS

INTRODUCTION 8
   ORIGINS OF THE OUIJA BOARD 11
   CONVINCING THE SKEPTICS 16
      OUT TO PROVE THEM WRONG *17*
      A MAN OF SCIENCE *19*
      THE BUS DRIVER *21*
   USING THE OUIJA BOARD ALONE 23
      LOCKED *24*
      SHATTERED GLASS *26*
      NOT THE CAT *29*
   UNEXPECTED GUESTS 32
      NEVER AGAIN *33*
      ALWAYS WATCHING *37*
      FOUR IN A ROOM *39*
   WHEN FAMILY CALLS 43
      BUBBLEGUM *44*
      BE WISE *47*
      DON'T WANT TO CROSS *49*
   ZOZO 52
      THE GATE *53*
      SCARED FOR THEIR SAFETY *56*
      A DEADLY OBSESSION *59*
   OMINOUS WARNINGS 62

- *24 JUNE 1987* *63*
- *DIE BITCH* *64*
- *HOW YOUNG IS YOUNG?* *67*
- WHEN SPIRITS ATTACK 69
  - *CECE'S FATHER* *70*
  - *LITTLE FLAMES OF LIGHT* *73*
  - *THE GRINNER* *75*
- BEST KEPT SECRETS 77
  - *WINDOW* *78*
  - *D-A-D* *82*
- THE DEVIL HIMSELF 85
  - *WOE* *86*
  - *THE FACE ON THE CEILING* *88*
  - *TWENTY WEEKS ALONG* *90*
- MOTIVE FOR MURDER 93
  - *THE OUIJA BOARD MADE ME DO IT* *94*
  - *MOTHER ON A MISSION* *95*
  - *A TORTURED CONFESSION* *97*
- POSSIBLE POSSESSIONS 98
  - *THE CAR ACCIDENT* *99*
  - *ALL I SAW WAS BLACK* *101*
  - *BELL FLOWER* *104*
- RELEASING THE DEMONS 106
  - *CURIOSITY CAN KILL YOU* *107*
  - *PORTAL* *110*
  - *N-O-M-D-E* *114*

SLEEP WELL **117**

INTRODUCTION

The Ouija board—probably the most infamous method of communicating with the "other side."

For years, and in countries around the world, supernatural enthusiasts have turned to the Ouija board for their first glimpse of what lies beyond—a dimension where ghosts, spirits, demons, and devils roam free.

With such a long and diverse history, it's unsurprising that Ouija has thrown up some interesting experiences. To some, it's just a bit of fun; a spooky parlor game to pass the time with friends. For others, however, the terrifying encounter haunts them for a lifetime; an experience never to be forgotten. These people would instantly erase their experience, if only they could...

For years, I've been fascinated by tales of the Ouija. This book is a culmination of my research to better understand the mysteries behind the *spirit board*.

Contained within is a brief explanation of the Ouija's mysterious origins. However, I know that you're all here for the spine-chilling stories! Don't worry, this book contains plenty, telling the stories of those souls brave enough to share, plus some of the most infamous events to come from the "game."

The stories challenge skeptics to become believers; deliver ominous warnings of the future; and uncover people's deepest, darkest secrets. All of this, made possible by one board, with 26 letters, ten numbers, and a few simple words. And a little help from the spirit world, of course.

Some of the stories have happy outcomes—for example, those seeking answers from lost loved ones, hoping to find closure. Take Karen, who got a final "I love you," from her grandpa, four years after his death. Or Brandy, who lost her mom to cancer—she found closure knowing that, even in death, her mom was always close by.

Other stories are just spooky—when the spirit knows everything about you, your life, your family, and all of your wrongdoings. This is what happened to Patricia; the Ouija board jump-starting a series of events that saw two men sent to a mental hospital and culminated in the death of her husband.

Then there are the strange events; flying objects, breaking glass, self-locking doors, and frightening noises in the night. They couldn't possibly be attributed to the Ouija board—could they? But these incidents are commonly reported after a session with the Ouija board, and a meeting with an unknown spirit.

As we progress through this book, the stories take a turn for the worst, becoming far more disturbing. Some spirits have a sinister agenda, and finding a living body to carry out their evil deeds is a top priority. One spirit haunted a young girl, forcing her to relive constantly the pain of the spirit's death. Other spirits can temporarily possess, causing the host to inflict harm on themselves.

And let's not ignore Zozo—arguably the most famous and often-encountered spirit using the Ouija board. Claimed by many to be a demon, Zozo appears for Ouija board users across the world and spanning decades. With every encounter, his infamy grows, and he is known for delivering catastrophic news. He also likes to toy with people, and even taunted one family for three generations.

These frightening stories must be told so that people understand the potential consequences of using Ouija to contact the spirit world. An encounter with the Devil might seem like a far-fetched event, though maybe most who speak to him are too traumatized to speak up. Still, some tales of contact with the Devil are included—possibly the strongest warning for anyone who thinks the Ouija is just fun and games.

No one knows why the Devil or any of his evil minions decide to make contact. Sometimes, he appears as a terrifying manifestation on the ceiling. At other times, he lurks in the background, waiting to deliver on a terrifying promise he made through the Ouija board.

Writing this book helped me to understand how unpredictable and diverse the spirit world is. But what struck me most is the power of the Ouija board to evoke the spirits. I realize that Ouija is so much more than the marked board it appears to be. Read on, and you'll discover more about Ouija's deep roots in spiritualism, and, hopefully, you'll walk away with an understanding of what a powerful tool Ouija can be.

As for the skeptics—just remember that most of us started that way. Until *something* changed our minds...

With that in mind, I hope you enjoy this book. And I wish you all a good night's sleep later!

ORIGINS OF THE OUIJA BOARD

For those curious about the paranormal dimension of our world—and the ghosts, spirits, apparitions and poltergeists that come with it—the Ouija board is seen as a useful, if not foreboding, tool to communicate with the beyond.

For the more skeptical among us, Ouija is a simple game—a popular entertainment choice for teenage slumber parties. No matter what camp you find yourself in, or even if you're on the fence, the modern day Ouija board actually has deep roots in American Spiritualism. Whether Ouija is a truly capable method of communicating with the beyond is up to you to decide.

In the 1840's, a new wave of Spiritualism was gaining popularity throughout the US and Europe. Based on the belief that spirits had important knowledge that they wished to impart on the living, Spiritualistic churches sprang up all over the country, led by mediums—people with a special connection to the beyond. No one knows exactly how Spiritualism began, but some historians believe that after the Civil War, people, in general, became more interested in the idea of communicating with the dead, since so many had lost loved ones during the fighting.

In the mid-1800s, Kate and Margaret Fox, two sisters and mediums living in New York, managed to contact and communicate with the spirit of a dead peddler. The story goes that they did this by listening to the knocks the spirit made on a wall and translating them into letters of the alphabet.

The sisters began doing public demonstrations of their communications with various spirits and became instant celebrities. From these humble beginnings, an explosion of tools to communicate with the beyond were soon developed.

'Table turning' was another method of calling on the spirits that soon became popular. A medium would sit with a group of 'sitters'—those who wished to communicate with the spirit world—who would all rest their fingers on the edge of a table and wait.

If they succeeded in making a connection with the spiritual world, the table would start to move, tilting and knocking its legs on the floor. The medium would then interpret the knocking as letters of the alphabet. Much like the wall-knocking method of the Fox sisters, this form of communication was very cumbersome.

As a way of dealing with impatient customers, some mediums would simply enter a trance to communicate with the beyond. However, many felt this lacked authenticity.

Other mediums adopted the use of a planchette—a heart-shaped device similar to the one you see in Ouija board today. However, instead of being used as a pointer, this planchette had a pencil attached to the end so the spirits could guide the medium's hands and spell out a message. While much more accessible and entertaining than the knocking method, people often complained that the spirits had terrible handwriting with the device.

The search for an effective communication tool continued, until, finally, the first 'talking boards' hit the scene.

It is unknown when the first talking board was invented—this is because most talking boards were made at home from scratch. However, in 1886, the *New York Daily Tribune* reported that people in Ohio were making talking boards— Ohio being a state at the forefront of the Spiritualism movement.

The boards covered all the basics needed for communication: the alphabet, numbers, the words 'yes,' 'no,' 'good evening' and 'goodnight.'

All of a sudden, talking boards were *the* tool to communicate with the beyond, and their popularity soared.

Tapping into this new found demand, in 1891, the *Kennard Novelty Company* patented one version of a talking board, with the intention of selling it commercially. They called it the *Ouija board*.

Many people mistakenly believe that the word 'Ouija' comes from the French and German words for 'yes'—'*oui*' and '*ja*.' However, in reality, the company adopted the word 'Ouija' from ancient Egyptian, meaning 'good luck.'

And so the Ouija board was born, with a selling price of $1.50 apiece.

Soon after in 1893, William Fuld took over the Ouija board, hoping to sell it to the mass market. No longer the tool of spiritual mediums alone, the board's popularity grew over the years, but Fuld was always cryptic about the Ouija board's working—he never publicly disclosed if, and, more importantly, how the board actually worked.

Ouija became a popular game to play on dates, mainly because it gave couples an excuse to sit together in the dark with their hands touching. Despite the game's apparent innocence, some people, especially mediums, became concerned about the board's secret powers.

With the release of *The Exercist* movie in 1973, the Ouija board's popularity exploded. In the famous first scene, a young girl becomes possessed by the Devil after playing alone with a Ouija board. Off the back of the film's success, many religious groups denounced the board as evil, claiming it was Satan's preferred form of communication.

Over the years, the Ouija board patent has been passed around—first bought by the Parker Brothers, and then Hasbro. As people's feelings toward the board changed, so did the company's marketing strategy. The Ouija board tagline was once, "*It's just a game, isn't it?*" Now it reads, "*Don't play Ouija if you think it's just a game.*"

Today, people are split between those who believe in the power of the Ouija board as a method of communicating with the dead, and those who think of it just as an entertaining pastime. However, time and again, skeptics and naysayers have been converted once they've experienced the Ouija Board—despite believing spirits can't communicate (or don't exist) they changed their mind once the spirits start talking, as they invariably do.

The planchette moves so frequently that researchers have studied the subconscious minds of people using Ouija boards. The theory goes that the players' subconscious minds guide muscular movements, which gives the impression that the planchette is moving of its own free will.

But even researchers don't think the subconscious explains *all* of the board's apparent powers. "I don't have any doubts in my mind that we can explain the vast majority of ostensibly paranormal experiences by looking to psychology," said psychologist Chris French. "Whether or not we can explain every single one is the $64,000 question."

Whether the planchette moves because of the player's subconscious or from the consciousness of a spirit with an urgent message, there are some stories of spiritual connections through Ouija that can't be explained as anything other than paranormal experiences. The rest of this book will take readers deeper into some of these experiences. Read on, and one thing's for sure: you'll never again think of Ouija as just a child's game.

CONVINCING THE SKEPTICS

For every person who believes in the power of the Ouija board, there are just as many who would never buy a word of it. Some of these skeptics doubt the board can be used to communicate with the paranormal world, while others simply claim there is no paranormal world to begin with.

Either way, such beliefs never seem to stop these skeptics from trying out Ouija, even if just to prove their friends wrong. However, things become really intriguing when these same skeptics—people who are willing to ridicule paranormal "nonsense" time and again—come to reassess their staunch opposition to Ouija and the paranormal after trying the board for themselves.

Some of them even become fervent believers. In my opinion, these are the people with the most convincing stories to share.

OUT TO PROVE THEM WRONG

One skeptic used to play the Ouija board regularly with his friends, but always complained that it was one of them when the planchette moved. His two friends were strong believers, so the skeptic decided to prove their guilt by blindfolding them while they played the game.

His friends agreed, and he secured them both with blindfolds, checking to make sure they couldn't see. The skeptic was confident that his friends wouldn't be able to move the planchette properly, and they'd have to admit the game didn't work. What actually happened was much more surprising.

The skeptic asked the board, "Is there a spirit here that wishes to communicate?"

After a moment's silence, the planchette slowly slid to "No."

The skeptic figured that his friends got lucky when they moved the planchette, but still he felt a chill run down his spine. He then decided to challenge his friends with a question that wasn't so straightforward.

"Why don't you want to communicate?"

The planchette moved, and spelled, "W-A-I-T-I-N-G."

To the skeptic's shock and fear, it hit each letter perfectly. Now, there was no way he could assume that his friends were doing the talking.

"What are you waiting for?" he asked next.

The planchette slid to "No," then spelled, "W-H-O."

So he asked, "Who are you waiting for?"

Again the planchette hit "No," then slid over "2-0-1-9-2-3-1." The response was precise, but made no sense to the skeptic.

"Who are you? What is your name?" he asked.

"S-T-O-P," was the spirit's reply.

The skeptic started to think that the spirit really didn't want to communicate with them, but still he wanted some answers. "Please talk to us."

"No," was the reply, followed swiftly by a *POP* of the bulb shattering in the lamp the boys were using. The room went dark.

The skeptic found a flashlight and a new bulb to put in the lamp. By the time he'd replaced the bulb, his friends had removed their blindfolds. On the table, the planchette hovered over "Goodbye." The friends swore again and again that they took their hands off the planchette right when the bulb blew.

The skeptic figured his friends were trying to spook him, and could have moved the planchette from "No" to "Goodbye" when he wasn't looking. But one thing was for sure: there was no way they were responsible for the spirit's reluctant communication with the blindfolds on.

A MAN OF SCIENCE

Educated in science and logical reasoning, doctors are probably the least likely people to believe in a spiritual world or the ability to communicate with it. They also witness death on a regular basis, and would probably have a hard time coping with the paranormal if they really did believe. Despite this, the Ouija board did manage to convince one young doctor that he may have contacted an evil entity.

The 30-year-old anonymous doctor found himself playing with a Ouija board one night, after his 22-year-old sister brought it over for some late-night, "scary" entertainment with a few friends.

The very first time the planchette moved, the group was contacted by a person who had committed suicide recently and had a message for someone in the room. The doctor and his sister were the only ones touching the planchette, and had no knowledge of this spirit or what had happened to him. Still, the doctor and his sister were able to act as mediums, delivering intimate details between the spirit and his friend, who was understandably very startled by the communication.

The group decided to give the board another try a different night, and found themselves communicating with a very energetic spirit who spelled ZAZA over and over, followed by SEX, and a series of gibberish.

Frustrated, they let the spirit be, but tried again the next night. This time the spirit spelled MAMA at an "alarmingly quick pace." They tried asking the spirit what that meant, and what its name was, but they never received a clear answer. The planchette zoomed around the board and made a figure eight. At one point, it counted down the alphabet backwards.

The doctor and his friends had had enough, and decided to stop. But when they took their hands off the planchette, it continued the gibberish message all on its own for a few seconds before coming to a stop.

After, the doctor felt that he had no choice to believe in the impossible, and became pretty weary of the Ouija board in general. Shocked by the experience, he worried that an evil entity may have been trying to communicate or even manipulate them through its nonsensical message.

A MAN OF SCIE.

Educated in science and logical reasoning, do
probably the least likely people to believe in a spirit
the ability to communicate with it. They also witness a
regular basis, and would probably have a hard time coping
with the paranormal if they really did believe. Despite this, the
Ouija board did manage to convince one young doctor that he
may have contacted an evil entity.

The 30-year-old anonymous doctor found himself playing
with a Ouija board one night, after his 22-year-old sister
brought it over for some late-night, "scary" entertainment with a
few friends.

The very first time the planchette moved, the group was
contacted by a person who had committed suicide recently and
had a message for someone in the room. The doctor and his
sister were the only ones touching the planchette, and had no
knowledge of this spirit or what had happened to him. Still, the
doctor and his sister were able to act as mediums, delivering
intimate details between the spirit and his friend, who was
understandably very startled by the communication.

The group decided to give the board another try a different
night, and found themselves communicating with a very
energetic spirit who spelled ZAZA over and over, followed by
SEX, and a series of gibberish.

Frustrated, they let the spirit be, but tried again the next
night. This time the spirit spelled MAMA at an "alarmingly quick
pace." They tried asking the spirit what that meant, and what its
name was, but they never received a clear answer. The

...ite zoomed around the board and made a figure eight. ...one point, it counted down the alphabet backwards.

The doctor and his friends had had enough, and decided to stop. But when they took their hands off the planchette, it continued the gibberish message all on its own for a few seconds before coming to a stop.

After, the doctor felt that he had no choice to believe in the impossible, and became pretty weary of the Ouija board in general. Shocked by the experience, he worried that an evil entity may have been trying to communicate or even manipulate them through its nonsensical message.

THE BUS DRIVER

One young man growing up in a quiet town was never interested in wasting his time with Ouija boards. One day, he saw a moving van on his quiet street and went over to introduce himself to the new neighbors.

This was when he met Anna, a beautiful girl. She was 18 years old, just like him, and lived with her two younger sisters, ages 16 and 13, and their mom. Anna and the young man became great friends—he liked her even though she was "into the boards." Her mom was a tarot card reader, and got all her daughters interested in communicating with the paranormal.

One day, the young man decided to invite Anna over to his home. Of course she asked him to play the Ouija board—some kind of game that was of no interest to him. But he agreed anyway, and soon enough Anna was talking to some spirit, asking all kinds of questions.

The young man became a little afraid of the whole thing, and the only question he really remembered Anna asking was, "So what do you do in life?"

Through the Ouija board, the spirit responded that he had been a bus driver.

So Anna said, "Show yourself."

The planchette moved to "Goodbye."

The young man never thought much of it after that, until two weeks later, when he discovered that Anna had been hit by a bus. She died.

At her funeral some time later, Anna's sister, Grace, approached him about the Ouija board. She insisted that she had been communicating with Anna since her death.

The young man said, "The spirit isn't her. Leave the Ouija board well enough alone."

Grace began to cry, and eventually convinced him to come over to her house so she could prove it. The young man wasn't surprised that the spirit claimed to be Anna. He didn't believe a word of it, but played along as it seemed to be giving Grace comfort.

Grace said to her sister through the board, "I wish I could see you again. Goodbye."

The session was closed; Grace and the young man never spoke about it again.

The young man was still a skeptic, until an accident at the end of the year convinced him of the Ouija's powers—and made him swear never to use one again. At the end of the school year, shortly after Grace got her driver's permit, she was hit by a bus and killed, too.

USING THE OUIJA BOARD ALONE

Many think the 1973 film *The Exorcist* was the scariest movie of all time. If you've seen it, you'll remember the very beginning, when a little girl makes a terrible mistake—playing with a Ouija board all alone. She ends up possessed by the Devil, and terrorizes everyone around her.

The movie has stuck with most of us, so much so that 'never use a Ouija board alone' has become the number one rule of contacting the spirits. If you don't follow it, horrible things might happen.

LOCKED

Sarah and her friends loved playing Ouija together, usually during the daytime. They would always call on this one spirit, named Ged, who told funny jokes and didn't make a whole lot of sense. For Sarah, Ouija was a fun experience.

One evening Sarah was alone in her room. Her friends hadn't come over that day, but she wanted to talk to Ged. She was also curious—secretly, she always suspected her friends might have been responsible for Ged and his jokes. If she tried it alone, she would know for sure.

Sarah got out the board and was contacted by Ged almost immediately. She thought it was pretty cool that he was speaking to her alone, and she didn't pay too much attention to the questions she asked or the answers he gave.

After a few minutes of chatting, the planchette suddenly stopped. "Are you still there?" asked Sarah, her hands still poised on the planchette.

It didn't move.

Just then the lights in her bedroom went off. Freaked out, Sarah ran to her bedroom door, thinking the power had gone out in the house. To her surprise, the door wouldn't open. The lock was on the inside, so she turned it back and forth, trying to get the door to move. It wouldn't budge, almost as if someone was holding it closed from the other side.

Scared, Sarah started yelling for someone to help her as she pulled and tugged on the door in the dark. Her sister heard her and came running down the hallway. She wrenched the door open with ease.

"What's the matter?" her sister asked.

"The door was stuck! Who was doing that?"

"I didn't see anybody," said her sister. "It opened just fine right now."

"Well…"

Sarah suddenly noticed the hall light shining behind her sister's head. The power hadn't gone out—all the other lights in the house worked fine except for the one in her room. Sarah burst into tears, unable to explain to her sister why she was so scared.

All she managed to say was, "I'm never playing Ouija alone again!"

SHATTERED GLASS

When Cameron was about 12 or 13, he was spending a lot of time home alone. His mother was in the hospital, and his father was working all the time. His parents were deeply religious, and absolutely loathed anything that might be considered evil, such as Ouija boards. But Cameron was curious, and decided to take advantage of his newfound freedom.

After making the Ouija board from scratch, Cameron sat at the dining room table with a glass of water. Hesitantly, he placed his fingers on the planchette.

"Hello?" he said.

Immediately, the planchette moved, slowly spelling out "H-E-L-L-O."

Cameron was surprised but excited, and decided to keep calm.

"What is your name?" he asked.

The planchette moved. "S-O-P-H-I-A."

Eager to know more about Sophia, Cameron asked another question. "Why are you here?" He deflated a little bit, because the planchette didn't move this time. After a minute, he tried a different question. "Are you trapped?"

Still, the planchette lay still.

"What do you want?"

Nothing.

"What do you need?"

No response.

Frustrated, Cameron was about to give up. Then he thought of something. "Are you a demon?"

In a swift jerking motion, the planchette slid to 'yes' and at the same time, Cameron's glass of water flew off the table and shattered on the wall behind him. Startled, Cameron jumped out of his chair, only to feel immediately dizzy. He was worried he might pass out, so he wandered out the front door to get some fresh air. That was the last thing he remembered.

When he woke up, his father's face was looming over him. He was still laying in the front yard where he'd fainted. His dad asked him what had happened, but Cameron kept saying he couldn't remember. He didn't want to tell his dad that he had used a Ouija board in the house.

When they walked back inside, Cameron saw that the Ouija board had disappeared. He walked wearily up to his bedroom, only to find that it had somehow been trashed. Books were all over the floor, some of them torn, and toys were everywhere—even the hallway. Cameron didn't know how that could have happened, but he didn't care; he was just too tired. He collapsed onto his bed and cleaned up the mess later.

Cameron vowed never to tell his parents about the Ouija board, but also to never use one again. He was sure he had drawn something evil into the house, and was only more certain as time went on. About once a week, he would open his door and find it completely ruined again. His dad thought it was Cameron lashing out, and Cameron never told his dad the truth.

NOT THE CAT

Kahla's Ouija board was homemade, because she, too, kept it a secret from her parents. Her mom had sworn them off Ouija—she had a bad experience with a talking board as a child, but never went into detail about what really happened.

Because her parents couldn't know about it, Kahla decided to play alone. She knew about the first rule of Ouija, but figured it was no big deal.

She tried to call on the spirits in her room one night. No one responded to her questions. Still she persisted, because she felt sure there was a spirit in the room. As soon as she put her hands on the planchette, the air thickened and the room grew colder. Despite the chills running down Kahla's spine, the planchette never moved.

Later that night, after giving up on Ouija, Kahla was lying in bed when she heard a loud *thunk* on the roof above. Seconds later, her dad opened her bedroom door.

"Did you hear something?" he asked.

"I think so..." she replied. "Maybe the cat?"

Thunk, thunk, thunk.

The sound returned, and it definitely wasn't the cat. It sounded like heavy footsteps, like an angry man stomping across the roof. Scared, Kahla ran downstairs, her dad shortly behind her.

"Mom!" she said, entering the living room. "There's someone on the roof!"

Kahla's dad ran into the back room and came out with a shotgun. He went outside. Kayla and her mom listened to him climbing onto the roof, feeling tense with fear.

A few minutes later, Kahla's dad came back inside.

"Whoever it was, they got away..." he said, shaking his head. "I saw a shadow jump down from the roof and disappear into the woods."

Kahla was freaked out, but couldn't bring herself to tell her parents that she'd used a Ouija board alone in their house. So instead, she marched upstairs and locked her bedroom door. She crossed the room and locked her window, feeling shaken.

Then she got the Ouija board out from under her bed, folded it in half with the planchette inside, and put a paper clip on it so it couldn't be opened. A flimsy solution, but what else could she do?

Kahla climbed back into bed and turned out the light. She lay awake, unable to sleep, thinking about the man on the roof and wondering where he had come from. Then a new sound came across her room. A growl.

Kahla sat straight up in bed. Again, she thought the cat might have been responsible for the sound, so she got up and looked around the room. To her dismay, the family cat was nowhere to be found.

Weary, she crawled back into bed, turned out the lights, and closed her eyes. The moment her eyes shut, the growl came again—this time louder, stronger and closer. Afraid, Kahla turned on the lights and left them on. After a long time sitting in silence, she slowly drifted to sleep.

Ever since that day, her house has been plagued by strange and threatening sounds, heard by everyone. Kahla began to believe that a demon was living in her home. Worse still, she knew exactly how it got there—through the Ouija board. Even with all the confusion and fear the sounds caused, Kahla never could tell her parents what she had invited into their home.

UNEXPECTED GUESTS

Most people who try using a Ouija board to contact the spirit world do so at home. Few realize that by doing so, they're potential inviting unwanted guests into their house.

Some spirits are harmless, gentle observers who do nothing more than give you goosebumps when you realize they're there. Unfortunately, others try to take advantage of your hospitality.

Here are three stories of unexpected guests people called into their homes with the help of a Ouija board.

NEVER AGAIN

Halloween night, 1968, and after trick-or-treating, Crystal thought it would be fun to bring a Ouija board over to Nancy's house for them to try.

The board gave Nancy the creeps. Nancy's mom was a psychic and she knew a lot about the occult. She thought the Ouija board was dangerous and told the girls to be careful.

Nancy had never played before, so Crystal taught her how it worked. She started by asking silly questions to the board, and the girls started getting appropriately silly responses.

"What was I in another life?" asked Crystal.

"You were a needle in God's eye!" the board replied.

Crystal swore she wasn't moving the planchette, but the board spelled out its responses so easily that Nancy was convinced she must be. When it was Nancy's turn to talk to the spirit, she decided to ask the same thing. "What was I in another life?"

"You were a nail in God's hand."

Nancy was bored with this stuff, and decided to try something different. "What boys do I like?"

The board replied, "Go to hell."

Crystal thought this was funny, and asked, "Okay, who will I marry?"

The board spelled, "You will marry the devil."

Nancy asked, "Is there a spirit in our house now?"

Then the girls were shocked to see the planchette fly rapidly across the board, "W-E-R-E-H-E-R-E." It took them a moment to understand what it said.

"What are the names of the spirits in the house?" they asked.

The board spelled out names, but the girls couldn't understand them.

"Where did you come from?" Nancy tried.

It spelled, "Hell. Where you're going."

The girls let out a scream, which brought Nancy's mother running into the room. Her mom decided she had a bad feeling, and asked them to stop using the board.

Quickly, Crystal asked another question, and the planchette started spinning across the board. Nancy's mom grabbed a pen and paper and started writing down each letter as it spelt, "We're here and we won't leave." Then the board started spelling out a string of curse words, followed by a message that made the girls' hands fly around with the planchette.

"Take your hands off it now!" screamed Nancy's mom.

Everyone was frightened and the room filled with a cold chill. Nancy's mother had a scared look on her face as she digested the news that the spirits weren't leaving.

Out of nowhere, a loud sound started banging on the stairs leading to the basement. Nancy's little sister Bonnie came flying into the kitchen. One look at her face showed she was frightened. On the verge of tears, she ran up to their mother, gasping for breath. "Something touched me downstairs! Something slapped my back. No one's down there Mom, and something slapped my back!"

Their mother gasped when she lifted up the back of Bonnie's shirt and found red marks on it. "And I heard a voice say something," said Bonnie, now crying freely.

"What did it say, Bonnie?" said their mom with false calm.

"It said, 'You hate your mother!'"

"It's okay!" said their mother. "Nothing is going to happen, but this is enough! Crystal put that thing on the coffee table and don't forget to take it home with you later. You three take a few minutes to cool down and just play. It's going to be all right, just go play."

Crystal put the Ouija board on the table and all three girls started to walk out of the kitchen. Just as Nancy was at the door, she saw something out of the corner of her eye—it flew across the sitting room, into the kitchen, went flying past her mom, and then crashed into the wall.

"What the hell was that?" screamed their mom. She looked under the table next to the Ouija board and found something startling—her camera, which was now broken.

Everyone was bewildered at how this could have happened. The camera had film in it, so their mom decided she would take it to the pharmacy to be developed the following day. They'd had enough fun for the night, so Crystal took her Ouija board and went home.

One week later, the film was ready so Nancy's mom went to the pharmacy and picked it up. All the photos were of a dark, hazy figure that looked like he was sitting on a smoky horse. It looked very strange. After showing the girls the photos, Nancy's mom said, "Never again will we have a Ouija board in this house."

ALWAYS WATCHING

One couple living in Alberta, Canada, decided to go to the toy store and buy a run-of-the-mill Ouija board for some afternoon fun. A little superstitious, they figured it was best to only use the Ouija board at 3pm, because this is said to be the time when Christ died, and the time that the Virgin Mary ascended to Heaven.

On the other hand, however, 3am is considered to be the witching hour. It's a time when a veil of darkness blankets the earth, and using the Ouija board at that time would invite communication with the most unholy of sprits.

The couple lived in a small basement suite and they were curious if any spirits might be sharing their home with them. Every time they used the board it worked, connecting them with some spirit from the beyond. They started using the board regularly to contact one particular spirit who liked to stay in their house. They discovered through the Ouija board that he was Pakistani, and his English was not very good.

They struggled to communicate while the Pakistani spirit kept spelling out a name over and over. It appeared to be a last name. So the couple decided to look it up in the phone book. Sure enough, the name was there, associated with their address. They communicated with the spirit again, and found out that he was in fact murdered in their home. He said he wasn't able to leave their basement home, but he was happy to be there.

The couple became curious if he was really in their home and watching them. So they decided to ask him what color their dog was. After a moment's pause, as if to study the dog, he spelled out W-H-I-T-E.

Next, they asked him what color the wife's hair was. He spelled M-A-N-Y. This was true—her hair had many different colors in it. They asked him if he was present in their house and if he was watching them. He replied YES.

The couple decided to take the communication to the next level, to see if the spirit would be willing to play copycat. The wife knocked twice on the table, then asked if he would repeat the sound. She and her husband then heard a very distinct knock—two times. They thought it was very eerie.

A few hours later, they tried to use the Ouija board, and were only able to contact the Pakistani man in their house. He was the only spirit who ever spoke to them now, but they didn't feel like he was dangerous. However, their house from then on had a certain strangeness about it, now that they knew there was someone else there with them—always watching.

FOUR IN A ROOM

Two friends found a Ouija board at a bookstore in downtown Orlando, and decided to buy it and give it a try. The two girls, Marta and Jenny, took the board home to Marta's house and managed to contact a spirit.

They asked the spirit many questions about his past, but then decided to change topic, and asked him how many people were in the room. The spirit replied that there were four. This was strange, because only the two girls and the spirit seemed to be present. So who was the unknown fourth person?

Both girls figured it was just the other one trying to mess around. They took their hands off the planchette, and just as they did, it started to move on its own, spelling C-L-O-S-E. They took that to mean that they should close the board, so they did. But first, they decided to say five prayers, asking God for His blessing of the house.

A few days later, Marta decided to tell her mom what had happened with the Ouija board. To her surprise, her mom was really upset and asked Marta to never use the board again. Apparently, their family had a bad history with spirit boards. Marta's mother told her the story.

Marta's grandmother had used a spirit board when she was in her 20s. She really enjoyed using it, and would constantly consult the spirits for advice; asking questions, and trying to get information about the world beyond.

She loved it so much that she became lost in the spirit board. She started to see things she couldn't explain: objects would move throughout the house, and she felt some kind of presence always inside her. The family decided to call in a priest to exorcise her of any spirits she might be carrying. It worked, and Marta's grandmother never played with the spirit board again.

Marta's mother had heard this story from her own mother, but never really believed it until she started playing with a Ouija board herself. She was also in her late 20s when her friend decided they should play with a board together. They had a lot of fun, sometimes making jokes and moving the planchette around themselves.

One time, though, they contacted a spirit who seemed very interested in her mother. It started asking her all kinds of questions about her mother, Marta's grandmother. Where was she? Why didn't she play anymore? Marta's mother became a little spooked, remembering the story her mother had told her. So she and her friend closed the board with some prayers.

But her friend was jealous that Marta's mother had managed to contact such an active spirit, and continued playing with the board. Then strange things started happening: objects started moving around the house, and the spirit seemed angry and agitated. She called in Marta's mother to help her, and they called on a priest to take the board and dispose of it. The two women never played again.

Marta, like her mother before her, didn't believe the stories. She and her friend Jenny continued to play and were always contacted by the same spirit, the good one who had told them to close the board before. Every time they contacted the spirit, they would ask him how many people were in the room, and he would always say three.

They asked him to warn them if another spirit ever entered, and he said he would. One time while they were communicating, the planchette started spinning, telling them to close, spelling the words EVIL, BAD, 4 IN A ROOM. Their curiosity got the best of them, and the girls decided to try and contact the fourth person.

"Who are you?" they asked.

"I AM," was the reply.

"Are you good or evil?"

The spirit didn't respond.

They decided to contact the good spirit again, but the new visitor wouldn't let him talk. For every question they asked, he kept saying "no." Just as the girls started to get upset about the strength of the spirit, he started asking questions about Marta. He said he felt like he knew her from somewhere.

Marta jumped away from the board, shocked. She knew who this spirit was. She ran crying into her mother's office, apologizing for never believing her. Her mother knew exactly what had happened. She took the Ouija board from the girls and put it in the living room. Jenny had no idea what was going on. Marta's mom left to get the Bible, and that's when the planchette started moving on its own.

It spelled, "I know who you are now."

Marta's mom returned. "Stop, I order you to stop!" she shouted.

Marta's mom sat down at the board; the girls sat terrified in the background. She didn't want the spirit to attach itself to either of the girls. She started reciting prayers, trying to cast the spirit away. "Do what you want to me but not my child. Not my child. You're not going to touch her." She called on God to cleanse the house.

That was when things went crazy. Objects started flying around and they could hear a strange sound—like someone was breathing hard in the room. Then, Marta felt someone slap her face.

Marta's mom became furious, placed the Bible directly on the board, and continued to pray to God. Marta joined her, and so did Jenny. They began to calm down as their prayers strengthened them.

After a minute, all the chaos ended. The energy in the room felt positive. Again, the planchette moved on its own. It spelled C-L-O-S-E. Immediately, the girls knew who it was: the good spirit. Marta's mother gently closed the board, took it away, and the girls never saw it again.

WHEN FAMILY CALLS

A lot of the time, Ouija board experiences are nothing but fun and games. Girls at slumber parties ask nameless ghosts whom they will marry, or maybe a spiritualist group learns the story of a long dead soldier who witnessed history.

In a lot of ways, communicating through Ouija can be very impersonal, though. You can't see the spirit you're talking to, and rarely do you spend enough time with them to really get to know them.

That is, until you chance upon someone in death who you knew in life. Is it a coincidence that lost family choose to call upon their living relatives? Or do they have a message, or some other unfinished business?

BUBBLEGUM

It was 1994, and Karen was going to college in Philadelphia. One weekend, a massive winter storm overtook the town, so everyone was holed up indoors. Karen and her roommate, Jen, decided to have a couple friends over to keep from going insane from boredom.

Once they were all together, Jen suggested that Karen get out her Ouija board. The other two thought it was a great idea—it would be fun to try and spook each other a little.

Jen and their friend, Mike, had the Ouija board set up between them. Almost immediately, everyone could sense a spiritual presence filling the room. The planchette moved before Jen could even ask a question.

"I W-A-N-T K-A-R-E-N," it spelled.

Karen sat in the background, looking surprised. She felt a shiver run down her spine.

Why me? she wondered to herself. Karen didn't like that the planchette had spelled her name, but since she wasn't actually the one playing, she figured it was safe to ask some questions.

"Who is this?" she asked.

The planchette spelled, "S-T-E-P-H-E-N."

Everyone in the room laughed—everyone except Karen. The others knew that Karen had a younger brother named Stephen, and thought it was probably a coincidence that the spirit had the same name. But what they didn't know was that Stephen was a family name. Her uncle was also named Stephen, and so was her grandfather.

"How do you know me?" asked Karen.

The room fell silent as the planchette moved under Jen and Mike's fingers. "G-R-A-N-D-P-A."

Jen looked up at Karen, confused. "Do you have a grandpa named Stephen too?"

Karen nodded. "He passed away when I was eight."

Everyone's attention drew back to the board. Karen had to know if this was really her grandpa, so she racked her brain for some early memories that only he would know about.

Finally, she said, "What was the special treat you used to bring me when you visited?"

The planchette moved to spell, "B-U-B-B-L-E-G-U-M."

Karen knew her friends couldn't have known that. Even her mother had probably forgotten. She leaned back on the couch, looking pale.

"What does that mean?" asked Jen.

Karen sighed. "When my grandpa came to visit me, he would bring me a cigar box filled with bubblegum cigars. We would sit together, he would smoke, and I would pretend to with the bubblegum."

The group stared at Karen. She was feeling pretty freaked out by this point, but reminded herself that this spirit had said nothing bad or harmful to her so far.

The planchette moved on its own. "I L-O-V-E Y-O-U," it spelled.

Karen hesitated. "I love you too, Grandpa."

Then the planchette moved to "Goodbye." The group decided to close the board.

Later that night, Karen was in bed when she suddenly remembered a dream she'd had when she was 12. Her grandpa had been gone for 4 years, but he came to her in the dream just to say that he was okay. Karen had asked, "Can I go with you to Heaven?"

"No," her grandpa said. "But I'm okay."

Karen had always felt close to her grandpa, and even after all these years, she felt he was with her always. She figured the dream and the Ouija board experience were his way of checking in with her and letting her know that everything was fine with him.

BE WISE

Eddie and his girlfriend, Denise, decided to try out Ouija together. Eddie had a specific spirit he wanted to contact, but he figured the effort was far-fetched. His father had committed suicide in 1993. He had been 38, and Eddie was just a little boy who had been left with more questions than answers about his father and his sudden death. Eddie had never told Denise what happened to his dad, but he still wanted her there for support, anyway.

When they set up the Ouija board in Eddie's room, they were surprised by how quickly a spirit contacted them. To Eddie's surprise, the spirit claimed to be Dale, his deceased father.

Eddie was amazed and immediately wondered if Denise had somehow known about his dad and was putting him on. He decided to ask some questions to be sure.

"What is your middle name?"

"J-O-S-E-P-H," the planchette spelled. This was true.

"What is Mom's middle name?"

"M-A O-N-E N-A-M-E."

"What does that mean?" asked Denise.

"My mom doesn't have a middle name," said Eddie, finally convinced about who this spirit really was.

"Do you have a message for me?" asked Eddie.

The planchette moved quickly—so fast that it pulled away from their fingers. "H-E-L-P M-A," it spelled. Then it moved again. "M-I-S-S M-A."

"Of course," said Eddie. "Anything else?"

The planchette moved to "Yes," then, "B-R-E-A-K U-P."

Eddie and Denise exchanged looks.

"What?" said Denise, looking upset.

The planchette replied, "B-E- W-I-S-E."

Denise was really upset, but Eddie was mostly bemused.

"Why should we break up?" he asked.

"N-I-C-K-O-L-A," the planchette spelled. "S-A-V-E H-E-R. L-O-V-E H-E-R."

"Who's Nickola?" asked Denise, rounding on Eddie.

"The girl I was with before you," he said somberly.

"Huh," said Denise, getting up from the board. "This is stupid. The Ouija board is talking nonsense."

"It's my father," said Eddie.

"It's not," said Denise, and she stormed from the room.

Eddie sat alone, the planchette unmoving, the spirit gone. He thought about his father's words. He thought about Denise. And he thought about calling Nickola.

DON'T WANT TO CROSS

Brandy's mom had died 3 weeks earlier from cancer. It was bad and she had suffered a lot, but Brandy still couldn't come to terms with the fact that she was really gone. So she decided to do something ridiculous and use a Ouija board to contact her, not knowing if it would really work.

Sitting in her mother's home alone, Brandy put her fingers on the planchette. "Mom?" she said tentatively.

The planchette moved to "Yes."

Surprised, Brandy asked, "Is it really you?"

"I-T I-S M-O-M," spelled the planchette.

Brandy was a little worried, because she had heard that evil spirits could sometimes contact people, posing as lost loved ones. Still, she felt she had no choice but to keep asking questions.

"Have you crossed over?" she asked.

The planchette slid to "No."

"Are you scared?"

"Yes."

"Do you want to stay in the house?"

"Yes," was her reply.

"Did it hurt when you died?" asked Brandy.

The planchette moved to "Yes."

"Were you scared?"

"Yes."

"I'm sad I can't spend Christmas with you," said Brandy.

The planchette moved. "I C-A-N S-E-E Y-O-U."

That was a bit of a scary thought, but Brandy moved on from it. "Do you have a message for Nana?"

"Yes, I L-O-V-E Y-O-U."

Brandy felt more at ease. "Well, if you're going to be here, can I get you anything for Christmas?"

The planchette sat still for a moment, then spelled "M-A-G-A-Z-I-N-E-S."

Brandy wondered how in the world she would be able to read them but said yes, anyway.

"What do you do all day?" she asked next.

"W-A-T-C-H B-R-A-N-D-Y."

"Do you have a message for me?"

The planchette moved. "B-E H-A-P-P-Y."

Brandy kept communicating with her mom for hours, becoming more convinced that the spirit was really her. Late in the night, Brandy said she had to go. "Sorry Mom, I'm tired."

The planchette moved. "A-N-O-T-H-E-R T-I-M-E."

Brandy sighed. "I want to talk to you all the time, but I'm still not sure if this is really even you."

"O-N-L-Y D-A-N-I-E-L-A," she spelled. Daniela was her name.

"Will you give me some signs when you're near me?"

The planchette moved. "B-E M-O-R-E A-L-E-R-T."

Brandy smiled. The planchette moved again. "I D-O-N-T W-A-N-T T-O C-R-O-S-S."

"It's okay, Mom," said Brandy. "Just stay here with me."

Brandy moved the planchette to "Goodbye," closed the board, and started getting ready for bed. She fell asleep easily for the first time in 3 weeks, knowing that her mom was close by, watching over her.

ZOZO

Anyone who has an interest in spiritualism and who uses the Ouija board has heard of the Zozo phenomenon. Zozo has brought terror to thousands of Ouija board users around the world. Despite this, it still remains unclear who, or what, he is.

Some say he's a figment of people's imaginations, perpetuated throughout time by colorful stories. Others say he's an evil spirit who's up to no good. Still others think he's a demon that guards the gates of Hell.

Read these Zozo stories and decide for yourself.

THE GATE

Deena was about ten years old when her aunt and uncle gave her a Ouija board when they visited from St. Louis. Like her family, Deena assumed it was a harmless game to pass the time. She really enjoyed playing with it and did so regularly over the years. Sometimes strange things would happen while she played, but those weird occurrences never scared her like they did her friends.

As Deena got older, she lost interest in playing with the Ouija board. Years later, when she was in her early thirties, she went back to her hometown with her two young children for a visit.

Deena's old friend, Murf, had passed away recently. She and her other childhood friend named Buddy went to Murf's house to say goodbye to his spirit. Buddy was a bit of a psychic.

When they arrived at Murf's house, Deena felt nothing. Buddy, on the other hand, instantly knew—"He's there, Deena." The two decided to go inside the house and use Deena's old Ouija board to try and contact Murf.

It was like he had been waiting to speak to them, because he responded immediately, moving the planchette quickly around the board. Deena and Buddy tested the spirit to see if he knew things only Murf would know. It was him, alright—the spirit even had the same sense of humor everyone had loved about Murf. He said he was happy, and the three of them communicated all night through the board.

The following night, Deena tried to contact Murf again alone. He wasn't there. Someone else, some other spirit, kept saying "Zozo is coming." Deena had no idea what it meant and kept trying to get the spirit to talk about other things, but all it continued to do was warn her.

That night, Deena lay in bed in her childhood home, unable to sleep. She heard the sound of footsteps in her room. Quickly, she flipped on her bedside light, terrified to see a dark figure sitting at her desk on the other side of the room. The dark man faded away in front of her eyes. Deena struggled to get to sleep.

The next day, she got online and searched for information about a Zozo spirit and the Ouija board. She found nothing, and didn't give it any more thought.

A few years later, Deena's now teenage daughter, Jill, brought home a fancy glow-in-the-dark Ouija board. Jill tried it out in the living room while Deena was getting ready for work.

Almost immediately, Jill was contacted by Zozo. The spirit said he had been waiting a long time for her to talk to him. He told Jill that her mother had opened the gate years before. When Deena entered the living room, Jill told her what the spirit had said.

While Jill spoke to Deena, the planchette moved again. "H-E-L-L-O D-E-E-N-A."

Disturbed, Deena told Jill to burn the board and left for work. Jill obliged, and it ended up being a wise decision. Plagued by the idea of Zozo, Deena did another internet search for the spirit. Now, strange encounters with the demon had appeared all over the Internet since she had last looked. All of them were nothing but terrifying.

Deena couldn't help but wonder how so many people had encountered the same evil entity she had learned of years before. Had she really opened the gate, like Zozo claimed?

SCARED FOR THEIR SAFETY

It was 2012, and April had just moved in with her sister, Joyce. One evening, the two sisters decided to have their friends, Trevor and Melissa, over to do something fun.

They were all having a smoke and pondering what to do when April suggested that they should play Ouija. April loved the idea of asking the spirits about the afterlife, and she had played with the board alone for many years without anything bad happening.

The four sat at the table together around the board. Joyce and the others weren't such strong believers, so April decided to lead the game. "Is anyone there?" she asked.

Slowly, the planchette moved to "Yes."

"Who are we speaking with?"

The planchette moved again, sliding to Z then O, then Z then O. It wouldn't stop moving between the two letters. It started picking up speed as it moved back and forth. Trevor and Melissa looked baffled.

"What do you want?" asked April.

The planchette moved quickly. "H-E-R."

"Who is her?"

The planchette moved again. "M-E-L-I-S-S-A."

Melissa smiled slightly, thinking it was a prank. April, however, was freaked out.

"What do you want with her?" she asked.

The only reply they received was "I W-A-N-T H-E-R," spelled quickly. The planchette didn't seem to want to stop, and returned to zipping back and forth between Z and O.

The group started getting fed up with this vague but energetic spirit. Frustrated, Melissa said, "This spirit's a prick."

Just as the insult left her mouth, the planchette halted on the board. Slowly, it began moving around again, spelling out "D-E-A-T-H."

"Why did you do that?" asked April. "He could be capable of doing something horrible to us…" She didn't want anything bad to happen to her friends.

Melissa sat quietly, a little shaken and ashamed. The others decided to try and continue to communicate. Soon, April noticed how warm the planchette felt under her fingers. In fact—it was getting hotter.

"Do you feel that?" said Joyce.

The others nodded.

"Are you angry?" April asked with a sense of foreboding.

The planchette started moving around so fast that no one could even keep up with the letters. Then the spirit seemed to get stuck in a rut, and started spelling "M-A-M-A" over and over.

April decided to try and force the planchette to a different letter but it wouldn't move. "Dammit!" she said.

Trevor pulled his hands away. "I'm done. This is too weird."

That was when the atmosphere completely changed. Nothing looked different, but April had the feeling there was a presence in the room. The air became heavy and fear crept into her eyes.

Suddenly, she didn't feel like herself anymore. Somehow, she knew that something was inside of her. From nowhere, a strong feeling of hatred washed over her. Then she started laughing—she had no idea why—and the next moment she was crying. She realized she had no control over her emotions anymore.

But that wasn't all. April felt the feeling of hatred creep in again, and found herself slowly turning towards Melissa. She smiled. It wasn't a happy smile, or a fake one—it was positively evil. April didn't feel like it was really her doing the actions; there was something inside of her, some demon.

Joyce slammed the board shut. "Trevor's right, this is getting creepy."

Everyone jumped up from the table, but April had trouble coming out of her reverie. She could still feel something dark boiling under the surface but didn't know what to say to the others.

After a while, she slowly started to return to normal. Once she completely felt like herself again, relief washed over her. She had been scared before, but not for herself. She was scared for the safety of her sister and their friends. April knew that whatever entered her body was powerful. If Zozo had wanted to hurt one of the others, she wouldn't have been able to stop it.

A DEADLY OBSESSION

Darren's first experience with Zozo was with a two-sided Ouija board he found at his girlfriend's house. One side looked normal, but the other side was dark and inscribed with the word Zozo.

Whenever Darren, his girlfriend, or any of their friends used this board, the planchette was controlled by this Zozo entity. Like many Ouija fanatics before him, Darren became a little obsessed with Zozo. He was determined to figure out what the spirit really was.

The more Darren communicated with Zozo, the more he started to think that he had been chosen by the spirit to learn the secrets of the afterlife. Soon, Darren realized that Zozo would appear no matter what Ouija board he used. The double-sided one wasn't special—Darren was. Nothing bad would happen to him.

As word spread of Darren's ability to call upon an apparent demon at will, skeptics in his quiet town outside of Tulsa began making their voices heard. Darren responded by taking a Ouija board to their houses and turning them into believers. One such time, Darren was with a group of people around the Ouija board. Zozo was repeatedly spelling the word 'window' and refused to stop.

Everyone was confused, including Darren, because there was nothing to see out the window. The skeptic herself went to the kitchen and looked out. Only then did she see him—a bald man staring in at her from the backyard.

The man was gone as soon as she saw him, but everyone was shaken. This was Darren's first time seeing a person appear while communicating with Zozo. Still, Darren kept calling on the spirit/demon, and over the course of five years, he began to feel more and more paranoid.

He became convinced that demons were taking on human form and following him. He had a nervous breakdown because of it, so his mom and grandmother intervened. They performed an exorcism to the best of their abilities, sending Darren into a deep sleep that lasted for two days. While he was out, his mother and grandmother witnessed dark shadows moving around the house.

Despite all the warnings, Darren felt he couldn't leave Zozo alone. He continued to communicate without telling his family. Then something really sinister happened.

Zozo told Darren quite clearly that he had plans to devour his daughter's soul. He said he would strike her down with an iron tongue. Frightened, Darren ended the session. But he didn't realize it was too late.

The very next day, Darren's three-year-old daughter nearly drowned in a bathtub. Later, doctors diagnosed her with MRSA. Her tongue became infected, and got so swollen that it dangled out of her mouth.

She spent two weeks in a hospital quarantine, but luckily she survived the infection. But this was the event that made Darren realize he wasn't special like he thought. Zozo had manipulated him into believing it. This was not a demon to mess with.

After this incident, he stopped using Ouija boards and spent his time warning others about the dangers of trying to penetrate the spirit world.

OMINOUS WARNINGS

Many people use Ouija boards to contact spirits: to learn about their lives, deaths, and what comes after. Others see the Ouija board as a kind of crystal ball that can deliver some truths about their own futures. No one knows how or why the spirits might know something about our lives, but then again we know so little about their world to begin with.

One thing's for sure—sometimes the spirits really do know something about what's in store for us. What we don't know is if there's anything we can do to change it.

24 JUNE 1987

It was 1986, and Jill had a very good friend at high school named Johnny. Johnny was suffering from cystic fibrosis, a debilitating illness. Recently, he had become very ill and was in the hospital.

Jill and her friend, Shelly, would visit Johnny often while he was sick. They tried to keep his spirits up, and kept hoping for a fast recovery. One evening after visiting him, they went to Shelly's house and decided to try a game of Ouija. Soon, they were able to contact and communicate with a spirit.

They asked basic and boring questions about the topics that preoccupied teenage girls—mostly about boys. That said, the spirit did seem to know quite a lot about the girls, including many of their secrets.

Jill decided to change the topic, and asked the spirit about Johnny and what was going to happen to him. The spirit responded quickly, spelling out "24 June 1987, Johnny won't have to worry anymore." Without waiting for another question, the planchette moved to "Goodbye."

Jill and Shelly were heartened by the message. Johnny had suffered so much from his illness—it was great news to know that it would all be over the following year.

They were convinced that the spirit had communicated a date for Johnny's recovery, so they wrote it down and put it in an envelope. The next year on June 24th, the spirit's prediction came true. Johnny didn't have to worry about his condition any longer—that was the day he died.

DIE BITCH

Angelina Jackson had always been interested in spiritualism and the occult—she often had dreams that became reality, sometimes devastatingly so.

When she was young, she dreamed her father wouldn't be around for Christmas. Soon after, he was diagnosed with cancer and passed away. Since that time, she grew more interest in spiritualism—regularly attending meetings and calling on the Ouija board. But when it came to messages from the beyond, she never seemed to take them seriously.

One time, Angela was at a spiritualist meeting about twenty years after her father died. A psychic woman got up on stage to sing and locked eyes with Angela in the crowd.

She sang a Jim Reeves' song, which was Angela's father's favorite. After she finished the song, the psychic spoke into the mic, her eyes still on Angela. "Your dad has a warning for you. You're thinking about using a Ouija board, but don't. No good will come from it."

Angela always knew that it was possible to connect with evil spirits or even demons with a Ouija board, and figured this was why her father warned her. But that didn't stop her from trying Ouija with three of her neighbors shortly after. They used an overturned whiskey glass as a planchette, which quickly began to move across the board.

"Who is it you want to speak to?" asked Robert, Angela's neighbor.

The whiskey glass moved across the board, spelling "A-N-G-E-L-A." Next, the spirit spelled, "Die bitch."

"That's not funny," said Angela.

"Angela, we didn't do anything," said Robert. Just then, the door to the living room slammed shut of its own accord. They all screamed and pulled their hands off the glass—all except Angela.

"Who are you?" she asked nervously.

"I was murdered," the spirit replied. "Just like you're going to be."

"Who are you?" she asked again.

"S-A-T-A-N."

Angela screamed, "I'm not scared—to hell with you!"

The group was done—they jumped up, turned on the lights and blew out the candles. "We should never do this again," said Robert.

But Angela couldn't let the ominous message go. She had to know more. She convinced them to try to contact the spirit again, but they were never able to.

"Then one night I woke screaming and sweating from a terrible nightmare. I'd dreamt I was being attacked by a man carrying a hammer. That's when I knew things had gone too far. I was scaring myself to death. I'm not doing the Ouija board any more, I vowed."

Still, Angela become increasingly paranoid, and felt unsafe going out. Eventually, she decided to visit her son who lived close by. She locked her flat and went down the stairs. That's when she heard the voice.

"Die bitch."

Shaking, Angela turned to see a man creeping out of the shadows. He wore a white T-shirt and had a claw hammer in his hand. "I screamed as he brought the weapon down on my head with a sickening thud. He hit me again and warm blood began trickling down my face."

Angela managed to get away and walked herself to the hospital in some sort of daze. The doctor saw immediately that she had been attacked. Her skull was fractured.

Later on, Angela told police everything she could about the attacker, but they never found him. She began to fear that he would come back some day to finish what he'd started. Six years later, she'd had no relief from her fears.

"If I'd listened to Dad's warnings through the psychic, maybe none of this would've happened. But now I'm warning all of you: never mess with Ouija boards. You don't know what evil lurks in the afterlife."

HOW YOUNG IS YOUNG?

Rachel, Sharrie, and Beth were like sisters. As teenagers growing up in Nebraska, they had shared a lot. Like many girls their age, one of their favorite sleepover pastimes was to play with a Ouija board. For them, it was nothing more than an entertaining game that gave them the spooks from time to time.

Sharrie kept a board in her bedroom, and they would call on the spirits to predict their futures—to tell them about boys they liked and other girlish things. Beth always had the most courage of the three girls, and sometimes would ask the spirits more serious questions.

One time, the girls decided to play the game at Rachel's house instead. They managed to contact a spirt named Yuri. But the fun didn't last long—Rachel's dad caught them playing. Being a religious man, he forbade them from the game and threw the Ouija board in the trash.

But then, after a few weeks, Rachel's dad came home yelling about the Ouija board again. He had found it in the garage sitting on the table, and was angry at Rachel for taking it out of the trash. Bewildered, Rachel never bothered to tell her dad that she hadn't moved the Ouija board. Instead, she decided to take it back to Sharrie's house, where it stayed.

The girls decided to play Ouija one more time after that. It would be their last. Sharrie was at a dance, so it was just Rachel and Beth. As usual, Beth got brave and decided to ask the spirit how they were all going to die. The spirit replied with something that Rachel would never forget. He predicted that both Rachel and Beth were going to die young.

"How am I going to die?" asked Beth.

The spirit replied, "In water."

This started to scare Rachel, but at this point Sharrie arrived to pick them up. Beth told her all about what the Ouija board said, but Sharrie just laughed and didn't take it seriously.

Years passed, and while the girls didn't see each other as much as they used to, they still remained close. They'd all grown up—Beth was married with a baby. Then one day a friend came over to visit Rachel and asked her to have a seat.

She told her that Beth and her husband had passed away. They were driving, hit a patch of black ice, and ran into a truck head-on. Both died instantly, but the baby survived. Beth and her husband were in their early 20's.

Rachel was overcome with grief and anger, but also fear started to creep in. She couldn't help but remember the Ouija board's prediction when they were all fourteen. The spirit had predicted that Beth would die by water: in reality—black ice. The same day, he'd predicted that Rachel would die young, too.

Still, Rachel's life went on. Sharrie was maid of honor at her wedding, while Beth was there in spirit. But even with her husband, children and busy life, Rachel couldn't help but wonder. How young is young? Thirty? Fifty? How much longer does she have to live? The thought still haunts her.

WHEN SPIRITS ATTACK

For a lot of people, the Ouija board seems innocuous enough. Even if they believe in the paranormal and spirits, what harm could come from communicating with them through a medium? Even if the spirits have sinister intentions, they couldn't possibly do any real harm on the living, could they?

CECE'S FATHER

Cynthia's father had passed away about nine months earlier. She was feeling pretty depressed, but her friend, Tanya, had been trying to cheer her up. So she reluctantly agreed to go with Tanya on a double date with Tyler and Nick.

They all went out to dinner together, and afterwards Nick had an idea that they should all play with a Ouija board. Tanya jumped at the idea, but Cynthia was hesitant. Reaching out to the spirit world after her father's death didn't seem like a good idea. Still, she didn't want to disappoint everyone, so she told them they could play and she would sit back and watch.

Back at Tyler's place, the guys set the mood by dimming the lights and lighting some candles. He, Nick, and Tanya gathered around the Ouija board while Cynthia sat in the back. Immediately, Cynthia could feel the oxygen in the room becoming thinner.

"Who do you want to speak with?" asked Nick, his fingers poised over the planchette.

The planchette moved. "C-E-C-E."

Cynthia gasped and jumped up. "That was my nickname when I was little."

The group stared at her. She hadn't known any of them as a child, and there was no way they could have known that her father had called her Cece.

"I wanna get out of here," she said. "I'm done."

"Relax," said Tanya. "Everything will be fine. Aren't you curious?"

Cynthia slowly sat back down while the others returned to the board.

"Who is here with us?" asked Nick.

The planchette moved across the board, spelling, "M-I-C-H-A-E-L."

"Liar!" Cynthia yelled suddenly. Everyone knew why. Cynthia's father's name was Michael.

Just as she shouted, all the candles blew out simultaneously. Tanya was the next to scream.

"I can't move my hands!" she said desperately. "They're stuck to the planchette!"

"Mine, too!" said both guys in unison.

Cynthia wasn't listening to them. She could feel someone squeezing her neck—some invisible entity was choking her. The pain was unbearable, and she fell to the floor, trying to call out to her father for help.

Lucky for Cynthia, she and Tanya had arranged for their friend Paul to pick them up at 8 pm. When he arrived, he heard screaming and struggling going on inside so he threw open the door and ran in. As he entered, he felt a strong gust of wind blow out the door, as if something was rushing out. Inside the house, everything had returned to normal. Cynthia's neck was free, and the others moved away from the planchette.

Paul took Cynthia and Tanya home. They didn't speak to Nick or Tyler again.

LITTLE FLAMES OF LIGHT

Mae was in her early seventies when her husband died. She didn't take it very well, and told her daughter, Jean, that she wanted to contact her husband's spirit. That was how she first started using a Ouija board at such an old age.

Mae had a lot of success and was able to contact many spirits, including her husband and members of his family. The spirits were friendly and made for great company, so Mae became obsessed with Ouija.

But after a while, something about the spirits changed. They would insult and abuse Mae. One time, they threatened to kill her.

Mae started to think that maybe these spirits weren't her husband's family, after all. She decided it was best to stop trying to communicate with them through Ouija, and she called Jean to tell her this.

Jean thought that was probably for the best. But after that phone call from her mom, she didn't hear from her for some time. Whenever Mae did call, the conversations were short and joyless. Jean lived far away, but she was getting nervous about her mother so she decided to go see her.

When she entered her mother's home, Jean knew something was wrong. Her mother looked troubled and tormented. When Jean asked her what was going on, Mae started saying strange things.

"The spirits are always around me," she said. "They're little flames of light."

Jean asked what the spirits said to her, and Mae repeated all the insults. Jean was sure her mother couldn't have known such horrible language. Worse still, Jean found cuts and bruises all over her mother's body. The spirits had been tormenting her in more than one way.

Jean moved her mother from the house and saw an immediate improvement in her health and happiness. Still, she couldn't fathom why anyone, spirit or not, would want to harm an old woman.

THE GRINNER

Lon was a high-schooler in the 1970s. One night, he went to a basement party at a friend's house. Tons of people were there from different schools and everyone was drinking.

In the middle of the party, a group of six was playing Ouija. Lon didn't pay much attention to the group until he heard some commotion.

"He grabbed my breasts!" said one girl sitting next to the Ouija board, looking very upset. "He keeps whispering in my ear and he grabbed me!"

The other kids in the group were looking around in confusion, but Lon noticed something else. A boy sitting across the table from the distraught girl was staring at her with a manic, evil look in his eyes. He looked like he might jump across the table at her.

Lon caught the boy's attention. "Stop!" he said.

As if on cue, the grinner rushed at Lon, his nostrils flaring with rage. He reached out his arms to grab Lon but he managed to roll away. Lon pulled the guy onto the couch and held him down. Seeing the commotion, several other partiers came over and helped Lon restrain the thrashing boy. Almost as suddenly as he attacked, he stopped, though.

"I'm sorry," said the boy, laying limply, all the fire gone. "I don't understand why I did that. I-I don't know what happened. I'm so sorry."

Lon and the partiers released the boy and watched him closely. Then a scream across the room caught their attention. Over at the Ouija board table, bewildered kids were watching in awe as the planchette hovered about two feet off the board.

No one was touching it, and people started backing away from the hovering object. Suddenly, the planchette slammed down into the board with so much force that it broke the wooden table underneath.

Everyone scatted, running from the house. This party was over.

BEST KEPT SECRETS

Some say spirits are all-knowing. It's true that sometimes people who venture into the world of Ouija will encounter spirits who know a lot about their past, or maybe a thing or two about their future.

But these instances could be chalked up to lucky guesses, or maybe their close friends were trying to spook them by dragging up the past. What's really strange is when the spirit seems to know something about you—some deep, dark, untold secret—that you never told anyone.

WINDOW

This story comes from Tulsa, Oklahoma. Dave and his wife, Michelle, decided to take an old Ouija board to their friends' house for some beers and fun. Mike had always believed in spirits, but Patricia was a skeptic.

The group decided to show her a thing or two about the power of Ouija. They got more than they bargained for, and by the end of the night, Dave and Mike found themselves in a mental health ward.

The group made themselves comfortable around a coffee table in Mike's living room, with dim lights and lit candles. Almost as soon as their hands touched the planchette, it started moving with force around the board, swooshing over 'Hello.' Patricia wasn't impressed.

They never got the chance to learn too much about the spirit they were communicating with, because almost immediately he started calling Patricia names.

As the planchette moved around the board, cursing at her and telling her he didn't like her, Patricia rolled her eyes, knowing the group was trying to get a rise out of her. Then, the spirit said something interesting. It claimed that Patricia was cheating on Mike with one of her ex-boyfriends. Everyone's interest piqued.

"Ask the spirit what her ex-boyfriend's name is," said Mike abruptly.

Dave and Michelle only knew Patricia through Mike, and had no idea who this ex could be. Still, they asked the spirit. His response was, "M-A-T-T."

Mike's face immediately turned red. But that wasn't all the spirit had to say. He went on to reveal that Patricia had been having sex with Matt earlier that day while Mike was at work.

"In which room?" said Mike calmly.

The planchette spelled, "Y-O-U-R B-E-D."

Patricia looked uncomfortable, but denied the spirit's message. Still, Mike jumped up and went to search the bedroom. He came back a minute later with a man's watch, saying that it wasn't his.

The planchette moved. "I W-A-N-T T-O S-C-A-R-E H-E-R."

Mike and Patricia started arguing and they abandoned the board. But eventually she talked him round and the group drank a few beers.

Everything was fine until Dave and Michelle decided it was time for a little more Ouija at midnight. They contacted the same spirit, who was still only in the mood to swear at and insult Patricia. Everyone thought it was enough and decided to end the night. Just then, the planchette spelled, 'W-I-N-D-O-W."

Everyone looked towards the living room window, but saw nothing. Still, the planchette spelled the word over and over, with increasing speed. "W-I-N-D-O-W. W-I-N-D-O-W. W-I-N-D-O-W."

Bored, Patricia decided to head to the kitchen to bring a round of beers. Then they heard her scream.

"Someone was looking at me through the window!" she yelled.

Dave and Michael ran out the front door to see who was out there. Sure enough, a tall figure was running down the street. They ran after him as he turned down an alley and disappeared into a building. Dave and Michael stopped dead, finding themselves surrounded by policemen and their cruisers. They were standing outside a mental health facility.

They quickly explained about the man who had been peering through the window of Mike's house. A hospital worker explained that the man had escaped from the facility somehow about an hour before, and that the cops had been looking for him. Mike and Dave waited outside, catching their breath, while the police went inside to talk to the man. When a police officer returned to tell them what was going on, he was laughing.

"The guy is definitely disturbed—didn't want to answer any of our questions. But he did tell the hospital faculty that the Devil had spoken to him. The Devil said he could find him at your house."

The officers thought this was very funny, but Mike and Dave felt chills after their evening with the Ouija board. They walked home to tell Michelle and Patricia what happened. Both women were scared, and Patricia wasn't happy. She threw the Ouija board out of the house and told Dave and Michelle not to come back.

Still, the guys decided it would be best to burn the board. After dousing the board in kerosene for good measure, Mike threw a match on it. But the board didn't burst into flame. Instead, it ignited a long flame that flew across the yard and then exploded in a giant ball of fire.

Mike was in the way of the blast and started screaming, burns covering his body. The others called an ambulance, and he and Patricia went to the hospital. He had second and third degree burns, and was temporarily blinded by the kerosene.

After the ambulance left, Dave picked up the Ouija board, which was still laying in the yard. The grass around it had been burnt, but the Ouija board was completely unharmed. Dave threw it in the trash can beside the house.

The next day, Dave received a call from Patricia. She was livid—accusing him of putting the Ouija board in the kitchen where the peeping tom had seen her. She wasn't amused. Dave tried to tell her that he'd thrown it away, but she didn't believe him.

After that eventful night, Mike had to have serious outpatient treatment for his burns. Dave and Mike stayed friends for about a year after that. One night, Mike told Dave that Patricia had eventually admitted that she was cheating on him. The Ouija board had all the facts straight—down to who it was and where they were doing it. Patricia may have been a skeptic before, but she couldn't be anymore. She learned the hard way—never play Ouija if you have a bad secret you want to keep.

D-A-D

Tom, Josh, and Chris were all friends. They had the summer off from middle school, and spent most of their time looking for some kind of trouble.

Tom was the oldest of the group, and always picked on Josh, the youngest. He was always pummeling Josh in the arm—as a joke, of course—but Josh would go home with bruises. Tom bullied him in other ways too, calling him stupid or retarded.

Tom just liked to be top dog, and Chris stayed out of the line of fire by keeping quiet. Still, when Chris and Josh were alone, they talked about how much they disliked the way Tom would act. But they had no one else to spend time with, so they tolerated it.

One day, the three boys found a Ouija board in someone else's garbage. Excited about the find, they took the board to Tom's house to play. His house was always the best place to meet, since no one was ever there. Tom had no brothers and sisters, his father worked a lot, and his mom had passed away some time before.

So the boys set up the Ouija board in the empty living room. They put their hands on the planchette and waited. And waited. Then they waited some more. Having the attention span of middle school boys that they were, they got bored after waiting about 20 minutes. They started discussing giving up—and that was when the planchette started to move.

It spelled, "G-E-T A-W-A-Y."

Tom wasn't impressed. "Get away? I live here!"

The planchette moved in a figure 8, then spelled, "N-O-W."

Chris looked around at the others. "That's weird. I wonder what it means?" He gave the board a confused look. "Where should we go?"

The planchette moved again. "I-T H-U-R-T-S."

Tom broke in, "This is stupid. You guys are doing this. Let's test it. Josh, let go."

As usual, Josh obeyed and took his hands off the planchette.

"Now ask it a question that only you will know," said Tom in a bossy voice.

Without a moment's thought, Josh asked, "Who's the person who keeps hitting me?"

Tom glared at Josh, but was quickly distracted because the planchette was already moving.

It spelled, "A-S-K T-O-M."

"This is stupid," said Tom again.

Then the planchette spelled, "D-A-D."

"Huh?" said Chris, staring confused at the board. "I think this question is for Tom." He and Josh glanced at each other, their expressions puzzled.

"D-A-D," the planchette spelled again. But Chris and Josh were becoming distracted by Tom's behavior. His breathing had quickened, he was sweating, and his face was beet red.

As if insisting they understand, "D-A-D," the planchette spelled again. At this point, Tom jumped away from the board and ran from the room. The other boys could hear him crying as he went. This was surprising, since neither Josh nor Chris had ever seen Tom cry before.

After a few days, they learned the whole truth about what the Ouija board was trying to tell them. Tom's father was abusing him, and instead of telling anyone about it, he was taking it out on Josh. No one could say how the board knew Tom's best kept secret.

THE DEVIL HIMSELF

Most people who sit down in front of a Ouija board expect to encounter some mysterious but benign spirit, or maybe nothing at all. More experienced, and maybe less fortunate, Ouija board users know to keep an eye out for malicious spirits or possibly even a demon from the netherworld.

But even *they* can be surprised by what they encounter, for few would dream that a simple Ouija board could bring them in contact with the most evil entity of all—the Devil himself.

WOE

Sam and Cherie were husband and wife, and they decided to try out the Ouija board for the first time together. They had never been interested in spiritualism before, but after they moved into their current home, Cherie began having strange experiences that she couldn't explain. She became sure that the place was haunted.

They invited their friend, Dania, over. She had a Ouija board and knew how to use it. Still, Sam was sure that nothing would happen.

They decided to set up the Ouija board next to a window where Cherie had heard many strange and unexplainable sounds. The three sat there for a minute—but nothing happened. So Dania asked, "Is anyone there?"

Immediately, the planchette moved to "Yes." Everyone looked around at each other in anticipation.

"Who is it?" asked Sam.

The planchette moved with ease. "S-A-T-A-N."

That was a pretty clear message, and everyone started to look worried. Still, they felt it was important to continue for Cherie.

"What do you want?" asked Sam.

"D-I-E."

No one really knew what to say next. Finally, Dania asked bravely, "Are you good or bad?"

The planchette spelled, "E-V-I-L."

Dania wanted to stop, but Cherie insisted that they had to get answers.

"What is your name?" she asked.

The planchette spelled, "W-O-E," then immediately slid to "Goodbye."

"Wait," said Sam. "We want to ask you more questions. What do you want from my wife?"

There was a pause while everyone sat expectantly with their fingers on the planchette. Finally, it moved. "S-O-U-L."

"Okay that's enough," said Cherie quickly.

They moved the planchette to "Goodbye" and flipped the board over. Everyone looked shaken.

"I don't think we should do that again," said Sam. "There are some things I don't want to know about."

THE FACE ON THE CEILING

Nine-year-old Sam and his sisters were a group of kids who liked to mess around with Ouija boards. One night they did just that, but it ended up being pretty boring, with no responses to any of their questions whatsoever. After about an hour of nothing scary happening, Sam and his sisters gave up and decided to call it a night.

Sam went to bed like usual and fell asleep quickly. But in the dead of night, he suddenly woke up to a freezing room. Shivering, he glanced over at his bedside clock and saw that is was midnight. Curling up tightly in his blankets, he rolled over onto his back to stare at the ceiling—looking at a blank surface was his favorite way to fall back asleep. But a blank surface was not what Sam saw.

Sam was horrified to find a face staring down at him from the ceiling, hovering above. He never had much of an imagination, but upon looking at it, he knew it must be the Devil himself.

The face looked exactly like the color of dried blood. It looked so much like a skull—its red skin stretched so tightly over it that Sam was sure it could rip at any time. The creature had no legs, but Sam could see a muscular torso behind the frightening face. Its eyes were not eyes, but burning lights that penetrated down at him. Two horns snaked out of the front of its forehead.

Petrified with fear, Sam lay quietly while the Devil smiled down at him in a malicious, even ghoulish way. He could see and hear the over-tight skin straining with the grin. Sam couldn't think of what to do, but he knew he couldn't stare at the creature any longer. He closed his eyes and began praying that the thing would disappear. He heard no sounds, but didn't dare open his eyes. After what seemed like ages, he fell completely asleep.

The following morning, Sam was relieved to find his bedroom devoid of devil-like creatures. Everything looked in order, but when he glanced over at his bedside clock, he saw that it still read 12:00 am. The digital clock wasn't flashing like it would be if there had been a power outage—it had simply froze. Curious, Sam pulled his favorite watch out of his desk drawer to check the time. The watch also read 12:00, down to the second.

Sam didn't tell anyone about his encounter with the Devil for ten years. To this day, the memory remains as vivid as if it had been the night before. Sam doesn't mess around with Ouija boards anymore.

TWENTY WEEKS ALONG

Dylan and Jake went to their friend, Mark's, family cabin one fall weekend. The three teenagers were looking forward to having the place to themselves, but didn't have too many great ideas about what they should do. Finally, someone suggested they try out a Ouija board. Everyone enthusiastically agreed.

The three boys were able to contact a spirt, but this one wasn't very friendly. All it wanted to communicate was that Jake was evil, and spell out "D-I-E" over and over again. The boys weren't amused and moved the planchette to "Goodbye." But then the spirit jerked the planchette away and spelled, "N-O D-I-E."

The boys kept trying to say goodbye to the spirit because they thought it was important to end the session. But every time they tried, the spirit jerked the planchette away again, telling them to die. They kept at it for a half an hour. Then Dylan had an idea.

"Spirit, show yourself!" he said to the board.

Immediately, the planchette slid to "Goodbye."

Just then, the front door of the cabin began to shake like crazy, then suddenly stopped. The boys went to dinner, not thinking too much of it.

Maybe it was curiosity, but later that night, everyone wanted to try the board again. When they sat at the board, they knew immediately that they'd found the same spirit. "NO" and "DIE" were the only words it was interested in spelling.

Mark thought it would be a good idea to try and ask questions about the future. "Will I have children?" he asked.

The planchette slid to "Yes."

"What about me?" said Jake.

The planchette moved again, spelling "N-O-W."

No one really understood what that meant, so they just kept asking questions. Mark and Dylan could tell that Jake was a little upset though, so they decided to stop shortly after. The three boys moved the planchette to "Goodbye."

The planchette jerked away. "NO. D-I-E," it spelled.

Then, the planchette started flying around the board, out of control. It flew off the board and onto the floor, where it lay still.

Dylan was the most superstitious of the group, and insisted that they couldn't let the session end without saying goodbye, because it might release the spirit to walk the earth. They had no choice but to continue talking to it. Still, everything they asked received only one response, "D-I-E."

"Who are you?" Mark finally asked.

The planchette moved to spell, "L-U-C-I-F-E-R."

That was too much for Jake. He got scared and ran from the cabin. The boys gave up on the board and went home the next day.

On Monday, Dylan went to school and saw that Jake wasn't there. He started asking around if anyone had seen him, then heard a rumor that Jake is in the hospital. The first thing Dylan thought was that something horrible must have happened to Jake, maybe by Lucifer himself.

Panicking, Dylan started calling Jake over and over. After several tries, someone answered.

"Hello? This is Jake's dad speaking."

"Hey! It's Dylan. I heard at school that Jake is in the hospital. What happened? Is he okay?"

There was a short pause at the other end before Jake's dad said, "Jake is fine. It's actually his girlfriend Tiffany who is in the hospital. She had a miscarriage."

Dylan was shocked. "A miscarriage? I didn't know she was even pregnant…"

"Tiffany didn't tell anyone, so we didn't know either," said Jake's dad somberly. "She was about twenty weeks along. It was a baby girl."

Suddenly, Dylan realized exactly what Lucifer was telling them through the Ouija board the other night. Jake really would have a child now, but in the worst possible way.

MOTIVE FOR MURDER

While the Parker Brothers would have you believe that the Ouija board is nothing but fun and games, the board has many times been the center of a much darker reality. Some people, especially religious groups, think that the Ouija board is a dangerous object, inviting evil spirits to convince or even force people to do horrific deeds. Others see the board as a way for people to confuse and distort their reality, giving their subconscious the chance to convince them to do something they would never otherwise do.

Regardless of the real reason, the Ouija board has a track record for bringing out the murderous side in the least (and sometimes the most) likely of characters. Take it from Mattie, a 15-year-old who shot and killed her father in 1935 after using a Ouija board: "The board could not be denied."

THE OUIJA BOARD MADE ME DO IT

Three boys between 14 and 15 years old met in a wooded area behind a high school in the small border town of Weslaco, Texas. All of them were friends and everything seemed fine, until one of them pulled out a 4-inch blade and stabbed his best friend in the stomach. The stabber then turned to his other frightened friend and asked for his help carrying the bleeding boy to a nearby garage. Shocked, he complied.

Once they arrived, the stabber said, "You gotta say that he fell on the knife so we can call an ambulance."

The boy agreed, but admitted the whole truth to the police as soon as they arrived. An ambulance took the injured boy to the emergency room and the stabber was arrested. When the police asked him why he stabbed his best friend, the boy simply said, "The Ouija board made me do it."

The police decided to look into the boy's history, and found no evidence of drug use or any mental health issues. They began to think that the 15-year-old attempted murderer really did believe the Ouija board was telling him that his best friend must die. Others, however, thought there was no way the boy would have done it unless he was somehow possessed. Either way, his murderous attempt failed—his former friend spent three days in intensive care but lived to tell the tale.

MOTHER ON A MISSION

One day, Carol Sue Elvaker played Ouija with her daughter, Tammy Roach, her son-in-law, Brian Roach, and her grandchildren. No one knows exactly what the Ouija board said to Carol, but soon after she went completely crazy.

Convinced that her son-in-law must die, the 53-year-old stabbed him in the chest. Then she decided her 10-year-old granddaughter was evil and tried to murder her, as well. Shocked by her mother's change in behavior, Tammy managed to get the knife away from her and hid it in the house.

It seemed like Carol had snapped out of it, and she offered to drive Tammy, Brian, and the family to the hospital so he could be treated for the stab wound. But soon enough Carol began driving erratically, and crashed the car into a road sign. She was intentionally trying to kill all of them, but she didn't succeed. Carol broke both of her ankles, and the others suffered small injuries.

The family got out of the car, while Brian was still bleeding in the back. Carol couldn't walk, but she wasn't deterred. She tried to push her other granddaughter, 15, into traffic before running into the woods nearby. She was later found by police and arrested, but that's not the end of the tale.

Her daughter Tammy was also taken in and charged with accessory to murder. She was the one who hid Carol's knife and owned the car they drove off in. Her husband never made it to the hospital—Tammy left him to bleed out after the accident. It turned out that Tammy was affected by the family's experience with the Ouija board just as much as Carol. Either that or the women were in cahoots to commit the ultimate crime.

A TORTURED CONFESSION

This story doesn't end with murder in the way courts define it, but someone still ends up dead.

It was 1935, and an elderly woman had weekly 'consultations' with her Ouija board about the doings of her 78-year-old husband, Herbert. The board was telling her that Herbert was having an affair with a woman in the neighborhood, and that he was giving her a lot of money. After each session with the Ouija board, the wife would stare darkly at her husband, telling him that she'd discovered the truth about more and more of his lies.

According to Herbert, his wife would then use wires to tie him to the bedposts and whip him with knotted ropes. She used a small knife to stab him in the shins and a hot poker to burn him, waiting for a confession. This went on for weeks, until the wife got fed up and put a gun to his head. Exhausted and scared, Herbert confessed to every crime she accused him of.

His crazed wife suddenly felt gratified and decided to untie him. Then she made a mistake by leaving the gun sitting on the nightstand. Herbert was traumatized and still terrified of his wife and what might happen after her next consultation with the Ouija board. So he took the gun and shot her in the back four times. When put on trial, the jury ruled it as a 'justifiable homicide,' since he was in fear for his life. The useful 'secrets' his wife had learned from her sessions with the Ouija board did nothing more than result in her own death.

POSSIBLE POSSESSIONS

Connecting with a spirit can be a tricky thing. If it were as simple as talking to someone, then there'd be no need for mediums to draw them out. But the scary question is: what does connecting with a spirit actually mean? Is it as simple as finding a way to speak the language of the dead?

Some say the connection is much stronger than that. The spirit must see your soul. Sometimes, they might just take ahold of it.

THE CAR ACCIDENT

Julie, Christine, Norah, and Tiffany were having a sleepover, and Christine suggested they play with a Ouija board. Julie didn't want to play—she thought it was too cliché, and also a bit evil, anyway. Christine, Norah and Tiffany didn't care though, and played for hours while Julie just watched.

They made contact with a spirit whose name was Gaby. She told the girls the story of her death. Gaby had died in a car accident—she crashed head-on into a tree and a branch impaled her in the stomach.

Soon after hearing the story, Christine started feeling strange. She started screaming and crying, saying she had extreme pains in her stomach and back. She could hardly breathe sitting up, so the other girls laid her down on a bed. She was resting, and there was nothing else for the girls to do. So they decided to play with the Ouija board some more.

The girls managed to contact a spirit almost immediately—it was Gaby again. "Did you do that to Christine?" asked Norah.

The planchette moved to "Yes."

"Why?" she asked.

Gaby responded, "I W-A-S M-A-D."

Just then, the planchette began flying around the board at top-speed, making a figure 8.

"Say goodbye," said Julie. "I think that means the spirit is evil."

Norah and Tiffany didn't listen. They were curious if this was really the same spirit. "What's your name?" asked Tiffany.

The planchette moved to 'H' and stopped there. It didn't move again.

Finally, the girls decided to say goodbye and close the board. Shortly after at their sleepover, they noticed that they all had bruises on their stomachs in the exact same place. Frightened, Julie got her rosary and Bible and the four girls prayed. Knowing that this spirit could somehow enter their bodies and harm them, they vowed never to use a Ouija board again.

ALL I SAW WAS BLACK

Josh had always been interested in the paranormal, which was why Ouija boards scared him. He thought it was best to be cautious with the spirits, and took the "don't ever touch a Ouija board, they're nothing but trouble" approach.

That was until Heather, his 13-year-old sister, begged him to play. Three of her friends, Jana, Chloe, and Shannon, were over for a sleepover, and insisted that the four of them weren't generating enough energy to attract the spirits. Josh agreed, though reluctantly, and spent an hour researching ways to protect against bad spirits online before beginning. Josh had the girls bring white tea lights and place them throughout the room.

The board was crudely made, nothing more than a piece of paper with letters and numbers written on it. The five of them gathered around the board, and Josh noticed that their positions made the shape of a pentagram. As a Catholic, this irked him, but he shrugged it off, not knowing what difference it would really make.

They managed to make a few contacts, but nothing particularly interesting happened. Then one spirit started getting very talkative before abruptly ceasing communication. The planchette stopped moving, and no matter what questions they asked, it wouldn't move. They decided to say 'goodbye' and try again.

Just then, the planchette moved sharply towards the edge of the board. Chloe screamed and pulled her hands away. Then suddenly, the planchette tipped sideways. Josh quickly took control of the planchette, moved it to 'goodbye,' and then flipped the board over.

Josh looked over at Heather and saw that she was wearing a look of shock. Maybe she was just scared, but she was staring directly into Josh's eyes: no blinking, no movement. Chloe decided to nudge Heather, but she didn't move.

"Are you okay?" asked Josh. "Stop it now, this isn't funny."

Still, Heather didn't respond. After sitting silently for a little longer, Heather suddenly gasped deeply as her hands flew to her throat. Her hands tightened. Somehow, she was trying to strangle herself. Everyone was shocked and didn't know what to do, but after about five seconds Heather released herself. She calmed down, her breathing slowed, and then she said, "What happened?"

"Oh, as if you don't know," said Josh, certain she was messing around and trying to scare them.

"No, I seriously have no idea. What the hell happened? All I saw was black."

This really scared Josh, but he knew what to do. He took all the girls outside and they ripped up the paper board, and then burned it. Once the board was completely gone, Heather told the others that she had a feeling of relief. "It's like a weight was lifted off my shoulders."

They went back inside, and Heather revealed to Josh that actually, this wasn't the first strange experience she'd had with a Ouija board. When Jana stayed over the last time, she and her mom were seeing ghosts in the house after playing.

Suddenly, Jana glanced towards Heather's bedroom. "I can see a man with no shirt on and brown hair. He just walked into your bedroom."

They all decided that was enough Ouija for the night. For Josh, one thing was sure: he'd never touch a Ouija board again.

BELL FLOWER

Sixteen-year-old Alexandra and her brother, Sergio, were visiting family in Mexico during the summer of 2014. They met up with their cousin, Fernando, and decided to play with a Ouija board to try and contact the spirits of Alexandra and Sergio's parents, who had died when they were very young.

In a community where shamanism is more commonly practiced than many would think, the orphans were told by their guardians to take *Brugmanisa*, a poisonous plant that locals call Bell Flower. It would bring them closer to the spirit world. The three took the drug together.

No one could tell you who or what they managed to contact that day, because after a few minutes of playing, they all appeared possessed.

Alexandra was the most affected. She started to growl and thrash, as if in some unbreakable trance. Sergio and Fernando started having hallucinations; that is, until they started to lose both their sight and hearing in a matter of minutes. Then, the three children started trying to hurt themselves.

"We tried to pray for them and to get them to pray, as well, but it only made the demons who had taken control of them angrier," said Maria Camaño, the guardian for the children. "I thought they were going to lose their minds. There is a lot of shamanism in the hills where we live and I was terrified when I saw what the Ouija had done to them."

Maria called on a Catholic priest to perform an exorcism, but since they weren't regular churchgoers in the town, the priest refused. She had no choice but to take the three to the hospital. Maria called paramedics, who had to restrain Alexandra to keep her from hurting herself or others. Shockingly, it was all caught on camera. She was speaking in tongues—in a voice no one could recognize.

"I'm going to die," Alexandra said in the ambulance, laughing.

"What are you laughing about?" the paramedic responded. "Why are you going to die? You have to get better, your family is waiting for you."

"They will die," she said.

"They had involuntary movements, and it was difficult to transfer them to the nearest hospital because they were so erratic," said Victor Demesa, the Tepoztlan director of public safety. "It appeared as if they were in a trance-like state, apparently after playing with the Ouija board. They spoke of feeling numbness, double vision, blindness, deafness, hallucinations, muscle spasm, and difficulty swallowing."

No one at the hospital knew what was wrong with them medically, so doctors gave them anti-stress medication, painkillers, and some eye drops. Slowly, Alexandra calmed down and the boys regained their senses.

What happened to the children that night with the Ouija board, we may never know—Alexandra, Sergio and Fernando don't remember. But Maria and the rest of the family are convinced they were possessed. Worse still, they think it's possible the evil spirits linger. Who can tell?

RELEASING THE DEMONS

Most people trying out Ouija are looking for a thrilling encounter with a long-dead spirit, or just a little fun and games with their friends. Few realize that they may be calling on something that isn't human, and never was.

The religious of the world have warned time and again that demons use the Ouija board as a gateway to your soul. If the subjects of these stories didn't believe it before, they certainly do now.

CURIOSITY CAN KILL YOU

Sam got his first Ouija board when he was thirteen. He was fascinated with the idea of communicating with spirits.

Maybe there was something special about Sam, because he was able to use the Ouija board all alone. His very first time, he contacted a ghost named Daniel. He was very friendly and easy to talk to—Sam would chat with him for hours at a time. Daniel had died long ago, and told Sam that he had a brother named Charles. But Charles wasn't like him. Daniel said he was mean, and liked to get into trouble. He was also close by.

Sam would talk to Daniel every day after school. Contacting him was so easy—he would just put his fingers on the planchette and instantly Daniel was there. But after each session, Sam would feel completely exhausted. He didn't realize it at the time, but his energy was being drained into the Ouija board.

One day, Sam came home and got out his Ouija board. "Is Daniel there?" he asked.

"No," was the reply.

Sam was taken aback by this—Daniel was always there. Then suddenly, he had a realization. "Is this Charles speaking to me?"

The planchette moved to "Yes."

Sam decided to talk to Charles a little bit, but proceeded with caution. As he communicated with him more, he realized that Charles wasn't as bad as Daniel had made him out to be.

Maybe he had a good side, Sam thought. Before long, Sam and Charles had developed a deep friendship. Now he was spending more time talking to Charles than to Daniel.

Ever curious about ways to communicate with spirits, one day Sam had an idea. If it was so easy to communicate with spirits by Ouija, what about by writing? He didn't know it at the time, but this method was called "automatic writing." Sam took a paper and pen, poised his hand, and attempted to call on the spirits. After only a few short seconds, his hand started to move on its own accord. Spirits could write through him.

With this new ability, Sam felt closer to the spirits than ever. He spent more and more time communicating through automatic writing—it was so much easier than a Ouija board. But as his connection with the spirits grew stronger, their messages became more sinister. Both Daniel and Charles spent a lot more time talking about death. The conversation often turned to the idea of Sam's death.

Sam was finally feeling scared, but also curious about the energy that was being drained from him every time he contacted the spirits. What else was transferring through this connection besides energy? One time, when he was angry because Charles kept talking about death, Sam decided to forcefully think of a random word while the spirit was writing. Surprisingly, that was the word that Charles wrote out.

Sam thought it was funny that he could exert some control over a spirit like that, but it also meant that the spirits had access to his inner thoughts when they were connected. Still, Sam kept trying to throw them off with these interjections. It only made them angry. More and more, the spirits were telling Sam that he should kill himself.

Sam couldn't help but continue to explore his rare spiritual connection, but eventually, he became fed up with the spirits constantly trying to convince him to take his own life. His mind made up, he took his Ouija board outside, broke it, and threw it away. He vowed never to try automatic writing again. And so, the spirits fell silent.

At the young age of thirteen, Sam learned a valuable lesson about contacting the beyond. Someone may befriend you and gain your trust, but if they steal your strength and try to influence you, then they must be evil deep down. Not all spirits are spirits, some are something more sinister. The most important lesson of all: too much curiosity just might kill you.

PORTAL

One night in college, John invited four friends, Liam, Chris, Jack and Paul, over to his apartment. The usual agenda was to drink and get into trouble, but this time they decided to change things up. They decided to have a séance.

At about 10:30 pm, the group decided that John would be the medium, since he was the host of the party. John brought out a Ouija board, and they improvised with a large whiskey glass for a planchette. Keeping true to what they thought a séance should look like, they turned off the lights and lit candles around the living room.

Liam was surprised to see how serious his four goof-off friends were about the séance. Everyone gathered around the board, for once completely serious.

John said to the whiskey glass, "If there is any spirit or presence in this apartment, please move the glass."

All were surprised to see the glass move immediately. They glanced around at each other before returning to the board.

"Would you be able to spell your name for us, please?" asked John.

The glass moved. "C-E-R-T-A-I-N-L-Y."

"What is your name?"

"I-L-K-E-R-L," it spelled.

"Ilkerl?" said Liam. "What kind of name is that?"

"Isn't it obvious?" said Paul. "It's an anagram for 'killer.'"

The guys cast around more nervous glances.

"Should we continue?" asked Jack.

"Maybe..." said Chris.

A discussion ensued, and the guys determined exactly how they should deal with the spirit. As long as they followed the right procedure and ended the session with a prayer, then they'd probably be okay. They read on the Internet that if the spirit mentions a portal, they should close the session immediately. Portals were how demons enter the human world. They all agreed to proceed cautiously, and not provoke the spirit. They returned to the board.

"If Ilkerl is still here, could you please make a sign?" asked John.

"OUCH!" yelled Chris.

"What is it?" said Jack.

Chris had his hand on his right cheek. "I just felt someone hit me."

Fear and foreboding spread throughout the room.

"Why did you hit Chris?" asked John.

"I D-O N-O-T L-I-K-E H-I-M."

"Why?"

"H-E I-S A T-W-A-T," the spirit replied.

Chris laughed it off. Maybe it was a joke.

"Are you a ghost?" asked John.

The glass moved to "No."

"Then what are you?"

The glass moved. "E-L P-E-N-U-M-B-R-A."

Suddenly, the room became ice cold. The guys didn't need to ask each other what 'El Penumbra' meant in English, they all knew. Demon.

"Ilkerl, are you a demon?" asked John.

The glass moved to "Yes," then, "N-O-W D-I-E."

Somehow, the room managed to go even colder.

"Oh my God," said Paul.

The others looked up to see blood trickling out of John's mouth. All five of the young men's faces filled with fear. Transfixed on John's face, it took a while for them to notice the glass and their hands, which were flying around the board.

"P-O-R-T-A-L P-O-R-T-A-L P-O-R-T-A-L P-O-R-T-A-L P-O-R-T-A-L P-O-R-T-A-L."

Their fears were confirmed—the demon was trying to enter their world. All five guys struggled to push the glass to "Goodbye." The demon resisted them, but they managed it. When they let go of the glass, it fell to the floor. The group recited "Our Father" and ended the prayer with "In Jesus' name, Amen."

They all rushed to turn on the lights and blow out the candles. John brought everyone some beer, and they tried to joke off the encounter. Still, no one felt they should leave John alone that night, so Liam, Chris, Jack and Paul all decided to sleep over. They managed to drink themselves to sleep.

Liam had a terrible nightmare. He found himself in a large room, in the middle of a circle of light. He couldn't see where he was because the room was billowing with a dark, smoky mist. He could hear high-pitched whispering in the shadows. Slowly, the whispers became louder—they became voices. Liam could finally make out what they were saying: "We're going to get you..." over and over. Then, the voices became screams. "WE'RE GOING TO GET YOU... WE'RE GOING TO GET YOU..."

Suddenly, hundreds of arms started appearing through the mist. Liam was paralyzed, unable to move. They were corpse-like, with talons on their hands. Liam couldn't see who the arms belonged to, but he knew that the corpses were the embodiment of Ilkerl. The gray mist started to creep into Liam's circle of light. With it came the dead arms. Liam had no way to escape the nightmare. He tried to scream, but it only came out as a soundless cough. The mist was surrounding him, the arms grabbing him.

Suddenly, Liam woke up, and found himself back in John's apartment. Four other frightened-looking faces were staring around the room. When Liam spoke to Chris, John, Jack and Paul about his nightmare, they discovered that all five of them had had the exact same dream.

N-O-M-D-E

One Tuesday evening, Amber was watching TV in her mom's living room. Daniel, her five-year-old brother, was falling asleep on her lap. Suddenly the doorbell rang. Amber gently pushed Daniel off and went to answer the door. To her surprise, it was her best friend, Dee.

"Look at my new board game!" said Dee, holding up a Ouija board.

"Cool, let's play!" said Amber, welcoming her in.

They set up the board in the living room and lit candles. Their fingers had barely touched the planchette when it moved to spell, "H-E-L-L-O."

"That's weird," said Dee. "It usually takes a while to respond."

"Creepy," said Amber. "How many people are in this building right now?" she asked the board.

The planchette moved to "6."

"That can't be right," said Dee. "It's only me, you, Daniel, your mom, and the spirit here."

The girls stared at each other.

Just then, Amber's mom came into the room and greeted the girls. When she saw the board, her expression changed.

"WHAT ON EARTH ARE YOU DOING PLAYING WITH THAT?" she yelled.

"It's not mine, it's Dee's—"

"Don't play, it's dangerous!" her mom said, then walked into the kitchen.

Amber and Dee looked at each other and both shrugged. "What is your name?" Dee asked the spirit.

"N-O-M-D-E," the spirit spelled.

Amber's face went white. "That spells Demon if you unscramble it."

The girls kept trying to communicate with the spirit, but now it had nothing but insults to throw at them. "Y-O-U B-I-T-C-H-E-S G-O D-I-E," it spelled.

Both girls screamed, waking up Daniel, who was still asleep on the couch. He screamed too, so Amber ran to him.

"The bad man tried to kill you in my dream, Ambey," he said.

Shivers went down Amber's spine. "Don't worry, I'm fine," she said.

Amber took David over to the board and sat him down. He wanted to ask a question. "Where are you now, ghost?"

The planchette moved. "I-N T-H-E K-I-T-C-H-E-N W-I-T-H Y-O-U-R M-O-T-H-E-R."

All three of them jumped up and ran into the kitchen, where Amber's mom was smoking a joint. "What are you kids up—?"

"Mom, the demon's gonna kill you!"

She shook her head. "Don't worry, that won't happen."

Just then, Amber felt something grab her hair and pull. She felt herself being pulled across the room, unable to stop the searing pain on her scalp. Dee also looked like she was being dragged around by her head. Amber's mom couldn't believe her eyes. She grabbed Daniel, got some blankets, and pulled the girls out of the house. They ran to Uncle Toby's house.

The family stayed overnight there. The next morning, Uncle Toby went to check out the other house. It was completely trashed. Everything of value was broken, but nothing was missing—no one had broken in. Knowing what to do, Toby took the Ouija board and burned it.

The family returned to the house and picked up the pieces. Things seemed normal for a while, but Amber began to notice things weren't quite right. Daniel began seeing shadows around the house and starting talking about a new imaginary friend he had. He said the imaginary friend was hurting him. Sometimes, Amber could feel someone touching her in the night.

A demon can do a lot of damage to a house after one night with a Ouija board. It becomes far worse when the sinister creature chooses to linger.

SLEEP WELL

The introduction of the Ouija Board gave the world a unique insight into what might lie beyond—for the first time, without needing to consult a medium or psychic. This gave people from all walks of life a potential opportunity to communicate with the world of the dead. As you can imagine, interest in Spiritualism and the paranormal skyrocketed.

What is it about those 26 letters and ten simple numbers that has fascinated generations? The simplicity and accessibility of the board are certainly important, but most of it boils down to the compelling—and sometimes frightening—stories being told by fellow Ouija board users.

This book has attempted to collect some of the most harrowing tales. If you're a believer, the stories have probably validated your view. If, however, you're a skeptic, perhaps this book has made you question your stance—with the sheer volume of stories coming from Ouija board users, many from skeptics, surely there has to be some truth and validity to it.

Perhaps we will never know the truth. All it takes, though, is a curious mind, a makeshift planchette, and the alphabet, and you can investigate matters for yourself. How about it?

DID YOU ENJOY *REAL HAUNTED OUIJA BOARDS?*

Again let me thank you for purchasing and reading this short collection of stories. There are a number of great books out there, so I really appreciate you choosing this one.

If you enjoyed the book, I'd like to ask for a small favor in return. If possible, I'd love for you to take a couple of minutes to leave a review for this book on Amazon. Your feedback will help me to make improvements to this book, as well as writing books on other topics that might be of interest to you!

OTHER BOOKS BY ZACHERY KNOWLES

Real Haunted Ouija Boards

Real Haunted Cemeteries and Graveyards

Real Demonic Possessions and Exorcisms

Real Haunted Woods and Forests

Real Police Ghost Stories

Real Haunted Castles and Fortresses

Real Haunted Hospitals and Mental Asylums

Real Hauntings at Sea

FREE GIFT REMINDER

Before you finish, I'd like to remind you one more time of the free eBook I'm offering to readers of my *True Ghost Stories* series.

To instantly download the PDF version of my book, *Real Black-Eyed Kids*, all you need to do is visit:

<u>www.realhorror.net</u>

Printed in Great Britain
by Amazon